D1524753

WORLD OF RACING

TRANS-AM®

By Sylvia Wilkinson

12073

Consultants:
Wiley McCoy
John Morton
Roman Kuzma

CHILDRENS PRESS, CHICAGO

Pace lap at Trois-Rivieres: Richard Spenard in 0, a Pontiac
Firebird Trans-Am and Paul Miller in 36, a Porsche 924 Carrera

PICTURE ACKNOWLEDGEMENTS

Jan Bigelow—Cover (front top, back cover 2 photos), 2, 4 (right), 5 (2 photos), 7
(2 photos), 8 (2 photos), 9, 10 (right), 11, 13 (3 photos), 15, 18 (2 photos), 19,
(2 photos, at left), 20, 22 (right), 29 (left), 32, 35 (2 photos), 37 (2 photos), 38
(2 photos), 39 (2 photos), 40 (2 photos), 41 (top), 42, 43 (top)

Michael Lufty—19 (bottom right)

David Hutson—Cover (front bottom), 4 (left), 10 (left), 17 (bottom), 19 (top right), 21
(2 photos), 22 (left), 29 (right), 31, 41 (bottom), 43 (bottom)

Wayne Hartman—16

Ford News Department—17 (top)

Jaguar Rover Triumph, Inc.—23

Pam Compton—25, 26, 27, 28 (all photos)

Yoshi Suzuka—30, 31, 36 (drawings)

Library of Congress Cataloging in Publication Data

Wilkinson, Sylvia, 1940-
   Trans-Am.

   (World of racing)
   Includes index.
   Summary: Discusses Trans-Am racing and explains how
Trans-Am cars are prepared for competition.
      1.   Automobiles, Racing—Juvenile literature.
2.   Automobile racing—Juvenile literature.
[1.   Automobiles, Racing.   2.   Automobile racing]
I.   Title.   II.   Series.
TL236.W53   1983   629.2'28   82-19721
   ISBN 0-516-04718-3   AACR2

A WOLF IN SHEEP'S CLOTHING

A Trans-Am® race car is a wolf in sheep's clothing. On the outside, it looks very much the same as a car on a showroom floor. But it is radically different.

Although the racing version of a Trans-Am car is a special machine, a street version must be available for people to buy from dealerships. The rules require that the car keep the same shape, but almost everything else can be changed. Even the body material can be changed from steel to lightweight fiberglass. Underneath its race car body is a wolf, a snarling, high-performance animal that has been carefully prepared for road racing competition.

 ®Trans-Am is a registered trademark of the Sports Car Club of America.

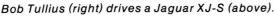
Bob Tullius (right) drives a Jaguar XJ-S (above).

This book goes to a Trans-Am race in Portland, Oregon, with frequent champion Bob Tullius, a motor racing veteran. We'll take a close-up look at how his team prepared his car to go from the showroom to the racetrack. Then we'll look inside the internal combustion engine. We'll discover what happens when a driver presses his foot on the gas pedal, creating a roar that is caused by as many as 48,000 internal explosions per minute! We will also understand turbocharging—a new development that will be very important in our automotive future. We will see how turbocharging is used to give a small engine much more power.

So off to Portland, where a pack of fifty ferocious Trans-Am wolves is ready to be turned loose into a peaceful city park!

4

GROUP 44

A beautiful race day dawns in Oregon after two days of threatening weather. But Bob Tullius, a driver who has won eighteen Trans-Am races, hasn't had a good weekend at the annual G.I. Joe's Rose Cup race. He was only able to qualify in fifteenth position in the large field, way behind his usual performance.

On Saturday, Bob told crew chief Lanky Foushee: "The car just isn't handling right."

Cornering action of the Jaguar XJ-S (below). Tullius discusses a handling problem with his crew (left).

Lanky combed through the car that evening, going down a checklist to make sure nothing was left undone. This was more than a routine maintenance check. He was trying to find the hidden difficulty that Bob had reported. Since the car had not responded to routine adjustments, he suspected a broken part.

Bob is proud of his team: "It's one on one when you're out there racing," he says, "but it's a team sport, too. If you have only 90 percent from your crew, you don't go the last lap." Lanky knows that Bob counts on him to make the car, which is capable of speeds of 185 miles an hour, as close to perfect and as safe as possible.

Finally Lanky's careful inspection paid off. He found a broken ball joint. A ball joint works much like a hip joint, a ball moving in a socket. A broken ball joint would keep the suspension joint from bending. The good handling will come back, Lanky thought, after I fix this. When he reported the discovery to Bob, the veteran driver smiled and went out to warm up the car.

"That was it," he reported happily as he drove back into the pits. Lanky showed Bob the lap times that verified his findings. He is faster now than a dozen of the cars that are starting the race in front of him.

6

Left: Lanky Foushee,
Tullius' crew chief,
talks with
Joe Huffaker,
builder of the
winning Pontiac
cars in 1982.

Below: Crew members
service the
race car.

George Follmer in his Chevrolet Camaro

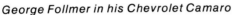

As Bob's team solves its problems in the warm-up, one of the teams on the front row suddenly is faced with a bigger problem. George Follmer rolls to a stop in his Camaro, his race engine blown. Caution flags go up as the once powerful motor pours oil onto the track.

George Follmer, like Bob Tullius, is a successful businessman, middle-aged and financially secure, but still racing. He often races against drivers half his age. When Bob Tullius was thirty, an age when many drivers think of retiring, he was getting even more serious about racing. What makes men like George and Bob want to take off three-piece suits and put on racing coveralls almost every weekend?

"Racing *is* my business. I was born to do it," Tullius answers. "But there is a contradiction. I have the successful racing business not only based on my ability as a driver, but on my ability as a businessman. In the early days, my driving had to support the business. One year I ran thirty-seven races. These days I have to dovetail my driving ambitions with my responsibilities to my business."

Bob admits that after a hundred career wins, "I don't get as much pleasure from racing as when I started. First it was a hobby. Familiarity with any occupation takes the edge off after a while, but I know there are millions of guys in nine-to-five jobs who would love to trade places with me."

Bob's team and business is called Group 44 Inc. No other team in America can boast of a more efficient operation. Group 44 mechanics are dressed in crisp, white uniforms, presenting the opposite of the greasy mechanic image.

Group 44 team in a rare relaxed moment

Spotless interior of the Jaguar XJ-S
(above) and the Group 44 truck (right)

"This clean, efficient image is extremely important to me," Bob says. "I grew up in the era of Jack Armstrong, the All-American Boy. Perhaps my mother caused my respect for a clean-cut image. Or the military. That part of my nature began to manifest itself when I was in the service. This is part of the reason our sponsors are satisfied clients. Our team has been together for twenty years, sixteen of them with Quaker State Oil. They know they can count on us for a first-class effort.

"Today everyone has uniforms, but we were pioneers. In 1966 we had six guys with Gant button-down collar shirts with Group 44 on the pocket. Every night at dinner we wore gold blazers and black trousers. We were the first team to have a big truck at the national races.

Backward Number 44 on deck lid of Jaguar

"I do remember when I was first attracted to beauty in a car. When I was eight years old, I had a friend whose uncle had a midget race car. It was beautiful. It had chrome on top of chrome. There were little swirls in the metal. I was attracted to the artistic value of that car long before I understood racing performance." One of Bob's proudest moments was when he heard Carroll Shelby, then the owner of one of America's most successful pro-racing teams, say, "I want our car to have clean wheels like Group 44."

People always ask Group 44 about the backward 44 on the car. "Years ago when a guy was cutting out numbers, he drew them on contact paper and forgot that when you're drawing on the backside, you need to reverse the image." The numbers are still used in reverse today, maybe to remind the team how easy it is, even for a first-class team, to make an obvious mistake.

THE RACE

When the green flag drops, Follmer, with a fresh engine in his car, and fellow front row man Greg Pickett, head off into a furious duel. Meanwhile back in the fifteenth starting position, Tullius begins to pick off the competition.

"The Jaguar is a big car in traffic," he has said, though he makes it seem small as he weaves in and around cars at a blinding pace. "I had one bad accident. But I have had a long career, over 250 races. You don't think about accidents when you're out there driving. They are just part of the business."

As he moves through the pack, he handles his race car with sureness. The car's good handling has returned, and with it, Bob's confidence. "I was turned on to driving cars when I was a teenager. As a little boy it was football and horses, but my father gave me a taste of driving back then even letting me steer and shift from his lap. I remember the first time I drove alone. I was hanging around a gas station on New Year's Day. This guy had a '36 Hudson, and he had gotten it stuck in the snow the night before. He said, 'Can you drive?' I said, 'Sure.' I took a Model A tow truck to go after it. The Hudson was on Maiden Lane in Rochester, New York. There was heavy snow on the ground with only two tracks for a car to follow. I drove that truck as fast as it would go in every gear."

Jaguar XJ-S (above left) and Canadian driver,
Eppie Wietzes in a Chevrolet Corvette (above right).
Tullius chases Chris Gleason's Camaro around a turn (below).

On the fourteenth lap, the race takes a major turn. Greg Pickett's Corvette motor explodes and he coasts to a halt. His race is over. The pace car rushes onto the track to slow the race so the stalled car can be moved to a safer area. After the spilled oil is cleaned up, the cars line up for the restart. Now everyone sees that Bob has moved all the way up to third place!

"I'll tell you how competitive life is for me," he has said. "When I walk down the street, I pass everyone I can. And I have a bad leg."

Bob's leg was injured playing football at an airforce base and he walks with a limp. "I have to admit that playing football, I was always frustrated because I had to play with ten other guys. I hadn't found myself. Then I got hurt and was disappointed. But I haven't seen three football games since I quit. Racing has been my life for twenty-five years."

When the green flag is waved to restart the race, Bob's experience pays off. He slips around rookie Tony Brassfield, and even surprises Follmer. Bob takes the lead with a frustrated Follmer a split second behind. Just behind him is Canadian Eppie Wietzes, who, like Tullius, made a charge from behind.

Tullius with winner's trophy

On the twenty-first lap, yet another front-runner falls by the wayside. This time it is challenger Follmer. He has run over some debris and limps into the pits with a flat tire.

"I knew Follmer was gone, but I couldn't let up. Wietzes was right there to nail me if I made a mistake."

Then luck goes Bob's way. A caution flag comes out to clean up another accident. Wietzes is trapped behind a slower car, so Bob gets the jump on the restart.

Bob takes the checkered flag in first place, only one third of a second ahead of Wietzes, one of the closest finishes in the history of the series. As he goes to the winner's circle for the nineteenth time in the Trans-Am, more than any other living driver, Tullius says with a smile: "Whether I'm a janitor or a race driver, I have two needs: One is to make a living and the other to satisfy a gigantic ego. Racing answers both of them."

HISTORY

The Trans-Am began in 1966 when the three major car manufacturers in the United States—Ford, Chrysler, and General Motors—and the Sports Car Club of America created a race series for sedan-type American sports cars or "pony cars." The pony cars were a new breed of high-performance cars. There was also a series for smaller foreign and domestic sedans called the 2.5-liter Trans-Am.

John Morton's Datsun 510, 1971-72 winner of the 2.5 liter Trans-Am

Boss Mustang (top) and Tom Gloy's 1982 Mustang (bottom)

Today the rules are carefully written so the American high-performance cars and the foreign sports and sedans race in the same group. No other racing series has cars with engines as small as two liters competing with cars as large as six liters.

Trans-Am racing, sanctioned by the Sports Car Club of America, puts into competition the best touring cars and sedans made in America, Europe, and Japan. These cars range from the costly Porsches of Germany and Jaguars of England to the familiar Trans-Am Pontiac, named by General Motors for the popular racing series.

Trans-Am cars must be mass-produced cars that are sold in the United States. At least one thousand cars must come off the assembly line every year for a car to be eligible. Also it must be a late model car, no older than five years.

In 1966, one of the popular pony cars was the Boss Mustang. A more recent example of a Trans-Am car from Ford is Tom Gloy's new Mustang.

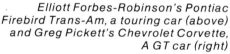
Elliott Forbes-Robinson's Pontiac
Firebird Trans-Am, a touring car (above)
and Greg Pickett's Chevrolet Corvette,
A GT car (right)

By definition the cars are two types: (1) *Touring* cars or sedans, designed to carry two to four passengers comfortably. This group includes American cars such as Pontiac Firebird, Dodge Aspen, AMC Hornet, Buick Regal, and Chevrolet Camaro; (2) *Grand Touring* (GT) or production sports cars, generally smaller, two passenger cars such as Greg Pickett's Corvette. Also a number of foreign cars are in this group: Tullius's Jaguar, Mazda RX7, Datsun 280Z, Porsche 911 and 924 Turbo, and the Triumph TR-8. Both touring and GT cars emphasize good handling and high performance.

A Trans-Am field contains cars that are very different in performance potential. John Bauer, 1980 Trans-Am champion, who races a Porsche 911, says: "Certain cars have the advantage on certain tracks." This means the smaller, better-

Start at Road Atlanta (above left),
John Bauer's Porsche 911 (above right),
Chevrolet Corvette, the only American
sports car (left), and Datsun
280 ZX, a Japanese sports car (below)

handling cars should do better on tight tracks, while the larger,
more powerful cars are at an advantage on fast tracks with
long straightaways. "The Trans-Am is a great mixing of cars.
This year there are fifteen good cars. Last year there were
only five. No one car dominates the field."

BUILDING THE RACE CARS

For racing to be exciting, cars must perform very similarly. If the showroom versions of the Trans-Am cars were raced, it would not be a fair competition because some are faster to begin with. It is up to the people who make the rules to keep the race cars competitive. The rules are written very carefully. They must be rewritten each year to include the new models.

Richard Spenard's Firebird and Ludwig Heimrath's Porsche 924 involved in an incident on the tight Trois-Riviere's track.

Power to weight

The main way that Trans-Am cars are kept similar is by close examination of the power to weight ratio. This is the amount of horsepower the engine produces versus the weight of the car. Simply put, it takes more horses to move a heavier load.

If the cars are made equal on paper, then it is up to drivers and mechanics to make individual cars faster by careful preparation. A better engine can be built and still stay within the rules. Also if a certain weight is allowed for the chassis, the challenge for the fabricator (metalworker) is to reach that weight and still have a car that is safe.

In Trans-Am Bob Tullius' Jaguar XJ-S has the largest engine (left). Doc Bundy won two races in this Porsche 924 (below)

Loren St. Lawrence in a Mercedes-Benz 380 SL, which is the racing version of a luxury car (above).

The Jaguar has a 12-cylinder engine (right).

While Tullius's Jaguar and the German Mercedes are both luxury cars, the Jaguar has a twelve-cylinder engine and the Mercedes an eight. Doc Bundy's Porsche 924 Turbo and Eppie Wietzes' Corvette are both production sports cars, but differ greatly in performance and weight. The 924 has four cylinders and the Corvette eight.

Here is an example of how Trans-Am rules attempt to equalize equipment with a power to weight ratio. Doc Bundy's 924 Porsche with about 375 horsepower has to weigh 1,750 pounds. Tullius's 530 horsepower Jaguar weighs 2,850 pounds. Tullius's car is 1,100 pounds heavier than Bundy's car, but has 155 more horsepower. This gives it a favorable power to weight ratio.

Although Tullius's car might seem very heavy for a race car, a Jaguar passenger car weighs 1,000 pounds more than the racing version. Let's look at what the Group 44 team did to turn a luxury car into a race car.

Weight

When Lanky Foushee, the crew chief at Group 44, prepared his first Jaguar for the team, he used a brand-new Jaguar. All of the comfort and luxury items that street car customers want are just excess baggage to a race team.

"I drove the car from the distributor in New Jersey to our shop in Virginia. There we stripped out the insides: floor mats, seats, door liners, door handles, window cranks, side window glass. We had to reduce the car to a shell before our real work began."

XJ-S Jaguar grand touring coupe is a street car

The 44 crew had to take 1,000 pounds of extra weight off the car yet still make the car strong and safe enough to meet racing standards. The mechanics follow a careful list of rules that outline what can and cannot be removed. For example, the headlights can be removed because all of the races are in the daylight and because they could easily be broken, leaving glass on the racetrack. The spare tire is taken from the trunk. Although a spare is important for a street car, a racing car must return to the pits to replace a flat tire.

The crew also rewelds all the seams of the basic chassis, strengthening it to take the stresses of racing. A special roll cage is constructed inside the car to protect the driver in crashes and rollovers. Today's race cars can even have a tube frame to replace the original structure. Fenders are flared so the car can use wide racing tires. A special, tight-fitting driver's seat is put in. A fire extinguishing system is added. The electrical, suspension, and brake systems are changed to meet racing needs. Many body panels that have been removed are replaced with panels of an identical shape made of fiberglass, a lightweight material. Then the crew adds the final "sheep" cover to the wolf: the green and white paint with a backward 44 on the deck lid.

Mock-up (a trial fit) of engine and front suspension to frame. Note the heavy channel iron table used as a bed to build the car. This is a precision level table called a frame jig or chassis table.

The cage structure around the cockpit is not only for driver safety, but also chassis stiffness.

Looking in from the rear (note back of driver's seat) we see the cross bracing of the roll cage that surrounds the driver.

The rear end (center) and discs or rotors (left and right) for inboard brakes are mounted in the chassis. (Note mock-up of driveshaft—bottom center)

The steel roof is permanently attached to the cage structure. A fender is trial fitted.

Looking from the rear,
the steel upper portions of
the rear fenders are added.

Doors, front fenders, hood, and front
spoiler are mocked up in a trial fit.
This is a difficult phase of construction
because all pieces are interrelated
and must fit perfectly.

All rear body parts are
being fitted. Note inner fender
panels still haven't been
trimmed.

Exhaust headers are being built.
This is especially difficult on a
12-cylinder engine because there
must be 12 pipes.

The right side of the exhaust
system is complete, making the
job half over. Note the six header
pipes go into one exhaust pipe.

Rear suspension with two springs
and two shock absorbers per wheel.

All fabrication has been completed on main chassis structure. Structure has been painted for final assembly.

Battery is mounted under left rear fender. Many heavy pieces are moved to the rear for better weight distribution on front engine cars such as the Jaguar.

The oil tank, a very heavy piece when filled, is mounted as far back as possible under the right rear fender.

Car is nearly complete. The fiberglass rear fenders have been installed and minor details such as taillights have been added.

Fire extinguisher bottle, fuel pumps, and oil filter bracket are mounted for installation.

Fuel cell is inside this metal box in the trunk. Notice two fuel pumps on left and related fuel hoses (called plumbing).

The Jaguar is ready for Trans-Am racing.

After many weeks of work, the chassis is race-ready, the weight problem solved. While the weight problem is being handled in the fabrication shop, in another room the engine builders work on the car's *power*. They build engines in a room as clean as a hospital operating room, so no trash will get inside and damage the smooth and constantly moving engine parts. When they're finished, they check the power of their engine on an apparatus known as a dynamometer, or simply, a dyno.

So, now let's consider that complex mechanism that brings the Trans-Am wolf to life—the engine.

Power

Every car depends on its engine to provide power. When Follmer's and Pickett's engines failed, their carefully constructed race cars rolled to a stop. To understand what happens when an engine ceases to work, we must understand what it is doing when it is working properly. Then we will talk to engine builder Wiley McCoy and find out how to make an engine more powerful. Wiley has built engines for many winning drivers: Richard Petty, A.J. Foyt, Tom Sneva, Johnny Rutherford, and Cale Yarborough, to name only a few.

Left: *A blown engine in Milt Minter's Firebird*

Below: *Doc Bundy goes wide to pass Eppie Wietze's smoking car*

Internal combustion

If combustion, the process of igniting fuel to produce power, takes place inside the cylinder of an engine, it is called an internal-combustion engine. The following diagrams show the inside of a cylinder on a normal four-stroke or four-cycle engine. Let's look at each of the four strokes.

On the first stroke, a mixture of air and fuel in vapor form goes into the cylinder. This mixture passes through the intake valve, which closes tightly when the air and fuel is inside.

On the second stroke, the piston rises and compresses the fuel/air mixture. This does two things to the mixture: it increases its pressure by decreasing its volume. If you take a partially inflated balloon and press it into a tight space, say under your foot, you increase the pressure inside the balloon. The second thing happening is increased pressure causes an

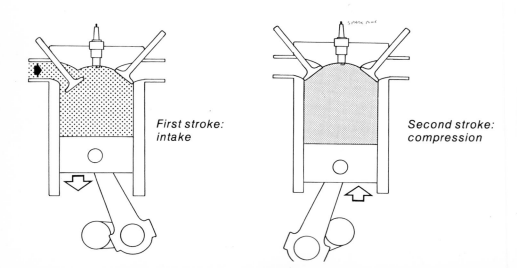

First stroke: intake

Second stroke: compression

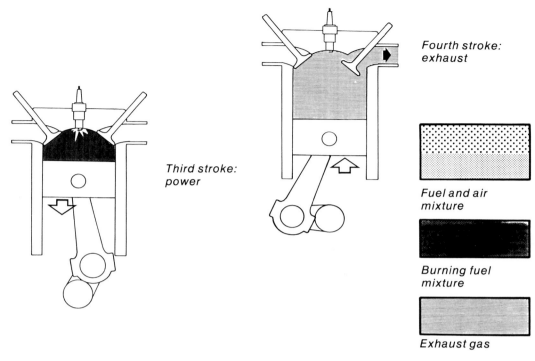

Fourth stroke: exhaust

Third stroke: power

Fuel and air mixture

Burning fuel mixture

Exhaust gas

increase in temperature. Have you ever pumped up a football with a small pump? The pump feels hot because as you compress air with it to fill the football, the air gets hot. On this stroke the fuel/air vapor is ignited by the spark plug at the top of the cylinder. Pow!

On the third stroke—the power stroke—the exploding fuel forces the piston down. This action turns the crankshaft. The turning of the crankshaft is the first step in a chain reaction that leads to the turning of the wheels.

On the fourth stroke, as the piston goes up again, the exhaust valve opens and the burned fuel is forced out. After this, the cycle can start over again: intake, compression, power, exhaust.

Energy

As you see, fuel provides the energy for the combustion process. When all the parts inside the engine are working properly, burning fuel puts energy into the system.

Each time the engine goes through the four strokes, the crankshaft turns two times. The crankshaft in Tullius's Jaguar engine turns over 8,000 revolutions per minute at top speed. It takes 4,000 explosions of fuel to make 8,000 revolutions. Since the engine has twelve cylinders, each with 4,000 explosions (or power strokes), there are 48,000 explosions per minute in his engine!

A variety of Trans-Am cars line up on the pace lap at Trois-Rivieres

Oftedahl Camaro climbs a hill at Mosport

This leads to our next question. How do we make an engine produce more power? And, we hope, without "blowing up" as Follmer's and Pickett's engines did at the Portland race.

When the inside of an engine is at the maximum legal size or displacement, using the largest pistons feasible, what is the next step for increasing power? Wiley explains: "The third stroke, or power stroke, is the only one doing any work. The first, second, and fourth strokes are doing negative work. The first, second, and fourth strokes use up some of the pressure made by the power stroke. To make more horsepower out of an engine, we need to raise the pressure on the power stroke. How do we raise this pressure? Fairly simply. We put more energy into the system. Our energy is fuel, gasoline in a Can-Am or Trans-Am car, alcohol in a Champ or sprint car engine. Since fuel won't burn without air, we have to put more air in, too."

A normal engine in a passenger car with a carburetor (called normally aspirated) isn't as efficient as a racing engine. It doesn't succeed in totally filling the combustion chamber with the fuel/air mixture on the intake stroke. The chamber is only about 80 percent full.

"When you are developing a racing engine, you are trying to get 100 percent air/fuel mixture into the engine," Wiley explains. "Finely tuned racing engines come close to what we call 100 percent volumetric efficiency at some speeds."

How does Wiley increase the efficiency? "Mother Nature hates a vacuum," he tells us, "so she fills the vacuum with air—the cylinder—through the intake valve. To get more air in than nature allows, we have to force it inside. This is where supercharging comes in."

A supercharger is an air pump. It takes in air, compresses it tighter than it is naturally and pushes it into the cylinder. With a supercharger on an engine, more fuel can be mixed with air because there is more air inside the cylinder. But, Wiley says, "The trouble with a supercharger is that it has to be driven off the engine by some mechanical means." That means it uses some of the power for itself.

Engine changes are often made at the race track.

Have you ever ridden in an air-conditioned car? When the air conditioner is running, although the passengers are more comfortable, part of the engine's power must be used to run it. Therefore, the car has less power to turn its wheels. This is how a better way of getting more air into the cylinder was devised.

"Before World War II," Wiley explains, "someone thought of spinning the supercharger with exhaust gas. There is a lot of energy, heat, and pressure coming out of an exhaust pipe. Why not spin a wheel with it? So the turbocharger was born."

35

Turbos

The basic idea for a turbocharger is simple—it works like a windmill, spinning as the exhaust hits its blades. But turbochargers have taken until now to catch on because of the need for strong, heat-resistant materials that come in contact with the hot exhaust gas. Only in recent years have we had metals that could withstand the heat and still do the job cheaply enough.

Turbocharging will be heard of more and more in the future on passenger cars. Turbochargers will be used because we need to conserve fuel and find a use for the exhaust gas that has been nothing but a pollutant.

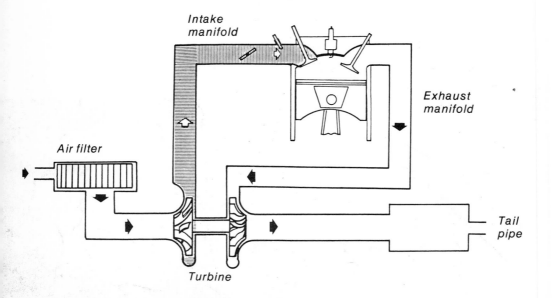

Driving a Turbocharged Car

Some cars that are equipped with turbochargers as street cars, such as the Porsche 924 and the Datsun 280Z, are used in Trans-Am racing. How does driving a turbocharged four-cylinder Porsche 924 compare to a car with an eight-cylinder (Corvette) or twelve-cylinder (Jaguar) engine?

Doc Bundy describes it: "First of all, it's only a four-cylinder, so even with turbocharging, it still lacks horsepower. You have to alter your driving technique to go quickly with a turbocharged car. I have to slow down before a turn, then nail it (give it a lot of gas) and keep on the throttle because I have to have exit speed at the end of the turn. A turbocharged car has to be tossed, manhandled, in the corners."

Doc Bundy (left) and Ludwig Heimrath, Jr., (below) drive turbocharged Porsche 924's.

A sad Doc Bundy (right) watches the wrecker remove his damaged car from the race track.

Doc holds up his hands. They are covered with blisters from holding onto the steering wheel in the turns. "I have to go into the turn deeper than most before braking. If I try outbraking them, they drive away when we leave the turn."

Since the car lacks horsepower, it is allowed to be lighter in weight. Asked if he felt threatened by the larger cars around him, Doc said: "The big cars shove me around all the time. The strongest point this car has is it's faster in the turns than the big cars. It is a constant speed machine, moderately fast all the time. The big cars have to slow down much more to make it through the corners, so that's my chance to pass. I love this kind of wheel-to-wheel racing. It's hard to imagine racing between cars that vary from 1,750 to 2,600 to 2,900 pounds. From my point of view, it's frustrating, but very challenging. And I know what it's like to get hit by one of the big guys!"

Driving a medium-sized car

Former champion John Bauer drives a six-cylinder, non-turbocharged Porsche. John explains, "My Porsche is a momentum machine. That means it is like driving a VW on the highway. You have to keep the speed up. If you let it drop, you can't put your foot down and accelerate back up to speed. To go really fast you have to drive the car on the ragged edge. With his V-12 engine, all Tullius has to do is put his foot down, on and off the throttle through traffic. But it always works out that different cars win every time.

John Bauer, the 1980 Trans-Am champion, gets a ride to the pits in another Porsche after his car (below) blew its engine.

"You know that the smaller cars should win on certain tracks with more tight turns," John says. "I should have won on a tight track like Lime Rock, but I didn't. Then I won at Brainard, one of the fastest tracks on the circuit. You find out that the conditions at each track determine the outcome of the race. At Brainard there was oil on the track which slowed the big cars down to my times. No one could go fast and the reason I won was I was the only one who didn't crash."

John Bauer sums up the Trans-Am: "I guess the beauty of Trans-Am is that it comes closer than any other form of racing to equalizing totally diverse cars."

The Brassfield brothers:
Tony in a Corvette (left) and Darin in a Firebird (right)

Above: Ralph Cooke in a Chevy Camaro
Below: Andy Porterfield, a former rodeo bull rider,
          drives a powerful Corvette

CONCLUSION

When you see a track filled with all the different kinds of Trans-Am cars—Corvettes, Jaguars, Camaros, Datsuns, and Porsches—each a different size and shape, remember that you know what is underneath their "sheep" coverings. You know that all of these diverse cars have something in common: each one is a carefully prepared "wolf," its engine and chassis made race ready by a team of mechanics. Each one, just like Bob Tullius's Jaguar, has been through the long hours of work and testing that takes a car from the showroom to the racetrack—ready for the Trans-Am!

Trans-Am cars tangle in a turn at Road America.

Above: Trans-Am cars jockey for position.
Below: Carl Shafer drives a Chevy Monza.

Glossary

alcohol: fuel used in sprint and Champ cars

back marker: a car/driver running near the back of the pack who qualified in the last rows of the grid

ball joint: a connector in a car's suspension that functions much like your hip joint—a ball in a socket

blown engine: an engine that has failed, usually with many broken parts. Examples: He blew his motor when he overrevved. The blown engine had a hole in the block. It also means a supercharged engine, using a blower to force air into the cylinders.

boost: the pressure of the air/fuel mixture entering a supercharged engine in excess of atmospheric pressure

bore: the diameter of a cylinder (see cylinder)

Can-Am: a North American (**Can**adian-**Am**erican) racing series for envelope bodied, 1,631 + pound, open cockpit cars using up to five-liter motors that are built for racing only and are raced on closed circuits

carburetor: an apparatus on an internal combustion engine that mixes fuel with air, sending it into the combustion chamber in vapor form by suction from the piston (see fuel injection for contrast)

Champ car: also called Indy or Championship car; a high powered, single seat, open cockpit and open wheel car used in North American competition, primarily oval track such as Indianapolis, some road racing

chassis: the frame upon which is mounted the body of a car, the understructure of a car. This is a confusing term meaning everything from a frame to a full car.

cockpit: the space in the race car where the driver is seated with access to the manual controls—steering wheel, gear shifter, brake, throttle, etc.

combustion: the process of igniting fuel in a chamber to produce power; the engine that works in this manner is called an internal-combustion engine

compression ratio: ratio between volume of the cylinder when the piston is down (or bottom-dead-center, b.d.c.) and when the piston is up (top-dead-center, t.d.c.)

cornering: the act of driving through a turn

crankshaft: a shaft inside the engine that, through the connecting rods, takes the back and forth movement of the pistons and turns this movement into the rotating movement of the driveshaft which turns the wheels

crew: the members of a racing team

crew chief: the mechanic in charge of car preparation who directs the individual members of the team, the "foreman" on a racing team

cylinder: a chamber in an internal-combustion engine through which a piston moves driven by the combustion process. Trans-Am engines vary from four cylinders (Porsche 924) to six (Datsun 280Z) to eight (Corvette) to twelve (Jaguar)

dashboard: a panel in front of the driver containing various gauges and switches

driver restraint system: a system of six belts that hook into a common buckle, two around the waist, two over the shoulders, and one or two through the crotch. This harness must be used whenever the vehicle is on the track.

dyno, dynamometer: an apparatus, usually placed in a soundproof chamber, used to measure the performance capabilities of an engine before it is installed in a car. Also used as a verb: He dynoed the engine.

engine displacement: the size of an engine, measured in cubic inches (ci, cu. ins.), cubic centimeters (cc.), cubic inch displacement (CID, c.i.d.), or liters, not including combustion chamber size

fabricator: a highly skilled metalworker who builds new structures (such as prototypes) or improves existing structures (such as GT or production cars)

fiberglass: fiberglass is glass in a bendable fiber form. When it is combined with resin and a catalyst (a substance used to cause a chemical reaction), it becomes fiberglass, a hard, lightweight substance used for race car bodies.

flags: internationally recognized signal system used in road racing, displayed beside the track by flagmen and/or corner workers. Examples: Green means start racing, checkered means the race is over, yellow means caution, red means stop immediately, etc.

flared fender: a wheel covering that has been enlarged to enclose a bigger wheel/ tire combination than is standard equipment on a car

flat-out: full throttle

fuel cell: the fire-safety container to hold fuel in a race car that consists of a metal or plastic structure with a rubber bladder filled with spongelike material

fuel injection: a pump and valve mechanism on an internal-combustion engine that sprays fuel directly into the combustion chamber. This more efficient means of supplying fuel for combustion is used on many race cars instead of carburetors.

GT: Grand Touring in English, Gran Turismo in Italian, Grand Tourisme in French. A GT car is a coupe with two or four seats made for street use, noted for good handling and comfort.

handling: the car's reaction to the manual controls, i.e., braking, accelerating, steering

headers: the part of the exhaust sytem that attaches to the cylinder heads to carry off burned gases from the engine. A performance improvement which replaces the more restrictive exhaust manifold

high-performance car: a car noted for its power and handling, in contrast to an economy car (inexpensive to purchase and operate) and a luxury car (comfortable, quiet, and expensive)

horsepower: standard unit of power used to measure engine output, equal to 746 watts and 550 foot-pounds of work per second

lean: engine condition, set for too little fuel to be used; a lean engine will lose power and can damage a piston from excessive heat (see rich)

manifold: a chamber that (1) takes the fuel/air mixture from the carburetor to the cylinder head (intake manifold) or (2) takes the exhaust from the cylinders to the exhaust pipes (exhaust manifold)

normally aspirated: an engine that "breathes" or takes in air for the combustion process without use of a turbocharger or supercharger (see turbocharger and supercharger)

pace car: a car used to lead the competitors in a race through a pace (or warm-up) lap, but does not participate in the race, pulling off the track before the green flag waves. Also can be used for a restart after a caution period (see flags)

piston: a hollow cylindrically-shaped piece, usually of aluminum, with a solid top (or crown) that is attached to a connecting rod by a pin (called a wrist pin); a piston travels back and forth inside a cylinder in an internal-combustion engine

pit, pits: The pit area is beside the racetrack, usually on a straightaway, and is used for refueling and servicing of the cars.

power to weight ratio: ratio of horsepower to weight of car

production: a car produced in quantity by a manufacturer

qualifying: an on-track session where a driver demonstrates his speed in relation to other car/driver combinations, determining his starting position and/or whether he can reach the speed required to run the race

racing slick: a wide, flat surface (treadless) tire used for racing only

redline: the maximum safe rotation speed of an engine, usually indicated by a red line on the tachometer dial. Some tachs (gauge that indicates engine rotation speed) have an additional indicator called a "tell-tale" (tattletail) that sticks at the highest revs the driver turned, tattling to the mechanics if he overrevved the engine.

revolutions, revs: revolutions per minute (RPMs) of an engine. Also used as a verb: Tullius revved his engine.

rich: engine condition, set for too much fuel to be used; a rich engine falters during acceleration, also lacks maximum potential power (see lean)

road racing: a form of racing that takes place on closed circuit tracks (in the U.S. from 1.5 to 5.2 miles long), designed to resemble a country road with a variety of turns and hills

roll cage: structure made of metal tubes used primarily in sedans (enclosed or "closed" cars) to protect the driver in a turnover by keeping the roof from caving in. Roll bars are used in open cars

scattershield: protective housing around the clutch and flywheel to intercept broken parts (shrapnel) should those components explode; to protect the driver and to keep broken pieces off the track

SCCA: Sports Car Club of America, the group that conducts Trans-Am races

spoiler: an air deflector sometimes used on the front and rear of GT cars to give downforce by redirecting airflow over and under the car

sponsor: a company or individual that furnishes the financial backing for a racing team

sports car: small, usually two-seat and open (convertible) car used for transportation on public roads, known for cornering ability and driving pleasure

stroke: (1) distance the piston travels in the cylinder (noun); (2) to drive slowly, conserving the car (verb)

supercharger: an air pump that takes in air, compresses it and pushes it into the cylinder; driven mechanically by the engine (see turbocharger)

suspension: the system of springs, shocks, and linkages that suspend the main structure of the car from the wheels. The suspension cushions the shock from an uneven road surface. It keeps the wheels in contact with the road so the front wheels can steer and the rear wheels can use the engine power efficiently.

torque: a measurement of force, while horsepower is a measurement of the ability to do work

touring car: in the Trans-Am, a sedan, an enclosed two to four passenger car, such as Camaro, Mustang

Trans-Am: a series of events for touring cars (sedans) and Grand Touring cars (production sports cars)

turbocharger (turbo): an air pump driven by the exhaust that operates like a windmill, giving the engine more power by forcing air into the cylinders, used to give a small engine much more power (for contrast see normally aspirated and supercharger)

turbocharger "screw": the device used in adjusting the amount of boost or pressure that the turbocharger forces into the engine (see boost)

V: engine design such as V-6 or V-8 where cylinders are arranged in two rows that form a "V" with the crankshaft at the bottom

valve: a mechanical device used to temporarily close a passage and/or to permit flow in one direction only of a liquid and/or gas

weld: to join two metal pieces by heating them to a fluid state and allowing them to flow together, generally by adding more fluid metal from a welding rod

Index

About the Author
Sylvia Wilkinson was born in Durham, North Carolina and studied at the
University of North Carolina, Hollins College, and Stanford University. She has
taught at UNC, William and Mary, Sweet Briar College, and held numerous writer-
in-residence posts. Her awards include a Eugene Saxton Memorial Trust Grant, a
Wallace Stegner Creative Writing Fellowship, a *Mademoiselle* Merit Award for
Literature, two Sir Walter Raleigh Awards for Literature, a National Endowment
for the Arts Grant, and a Guggenheim Fellowship. In addition to four novels, she
has written a nonfiction work on auto racing: *The Stainless Steel Carrot;* an
adventure series on auto racing; an education handbook; and articles for *Sports
Illustrated, Mademoiselle, Ingenue, True, The American Scholar, The Writer,* and others.
She has published five novels. *Moss on the North Side, A Killing Frost, Cale,* and
Shadow of the Mountain are available in Pocket editions. Her fifth novel, *Bone of My
Bones,* was published by G.P. Putnam's.
  Sylvia Wilkinson was head timer and scorer for Paul Newman's Can-Am racing
team and has worked with many other professional racing teams.